The Irish Village

The Irish Village

PHOTOGRAPHS BY ROBIN MORRISON

Commentaries by Christopher Fitz-Simon

with 150 colour photographs

THAMES AND HUDSON

Below Larry Whelan (behind the bar) owns this pub in Blackwater, Co. Wexford, from which the venerable locals observe the frenzied comings and goings of summer campers and caravaners. Seated from left to right are Patrick Corrigan (aged 78), James Foley (77) and Nick Leacy (84).

Half-title Shell-work, like these harp and shamrock motifs in Blackwater, is a recognized form of folk art on the south-east coast of Ireland.

Title page The River Blackwater at Benburb, Co. Tyrone, where General Eoin Ruadh O'Neill defeated a Scots and English force under General Monroe in 1646: Ireland's last great victory over the invader.

Contents page Castletownshend, Co. Cork, home village for Edith Somerville, co-author of the *Irish R. M.* stories.

Printed and bound in Japan by Dai Nippon

Contents

Introduction
6

Map of Ireland
10

The Villages
12

Introduction

There is an ease in travelling through Ireland which allows photographing the villages to be a far more pleasurable undertaking than it would be in most places. There are few of the physical problems of the more industrialized countries – crowded motorways or frustrating parking restrictions; but, more than that, the friendliness, warmth and help offered to the traveller make the going easy.

I had always wanted to photograph in Ireland – I suspect because of a vague sentimental attachment to a country from which one side of my family originally came, though also because of the literature and a love of Yeats and Joyce. As a fifth-generation New Zealander, I see Ireland as an outsider, but I do have a feeling for my Celtic origins and an interest in what makes up my own culture. In the sixties I spent an Easter in Dublin, soaking up the atmosphere I had perceived in the novels and short stories of James Joyce – even going as far as to sleep on a park bench in St Stephen's Green (an uncomfortable night, only partly softened by my introduction to Guinness).

I have shown the Irish village as it seems to me. I have enjoyed photographing the romantic, but I have also photographed with a documentary eye, being aware that village life evolves and that as ways of life disappear, a record of everyday happenings becomes invaluable.

The Irish village has avoided the embalmed prettiness that typifies the Cotswold villages of England, for example. In Ireland, villages are working communities and although many depend for their livelihood on the seasonal tourist trade, there is certainly little evidence of the commercialism that has scarred many other countries.

Irish emigrants have of course taken something of their culture with them, and when their descendants visit Ireland, they discover for themselves aspects of their own lives that they realize to be Irish – from the way they spend their leisure, to the colours they

Shop windows from (*top, left to right*) Louisburgh, Co. Mayo; Louisburgh, Co. Mayo; Castlegregory, Co. Kerry; (*bottom, left to right*) Broadford, Co. Clare; Dromahair, Co. Leitrim.

paint their houses. In the south of the Republic, particularly in Counties Clare, Kerry and Cork, the vibrant colours of the cottages made me understand where the fascination for brightly painted houses in my own country has its origins. This love of colour is certainly not an English or a Scottish trait.

At different times during the Spring and Summer of 1985, I travelled all over Ireland, stopping and photographing what caught my eye. I chose not to photograph the suffering caused by political and religious intransigence, and have illustrated those aspects which I think give a feel of the Irish village in its many different forms.

The greatest pleasure of travelling in Ireland is the meeting of people, and the best place to meet people is in their villages, where life is slower and there is time to sit and talk and discover Ireland in your own way.

ROBIN MORRISON

Acknowledgments

Much of the information in this book has been checked against entries in *The Shell Guide to Ireland* by Lord Killanin and Michael V. Duignan (Ebury Press), *Discover Northern Ireland* by Ernest Sandford (Northern Ireland Tourist Board), *The Ireland Guide* (Bord Fáilte/Irish Tourist Board) and *Ireland Observed* by Maurice Craig and the Knight of Glin (The Mercier Press).

Opposite Electricity reached all parts of rural Ireland several decades before a piped water supply was made available to every home. The ubiquitous 'parish pump', though less and less used, is still to be seen in many villages. When finally made redundant, pumps are eagerly seized upon as adornments for suburban gardens.

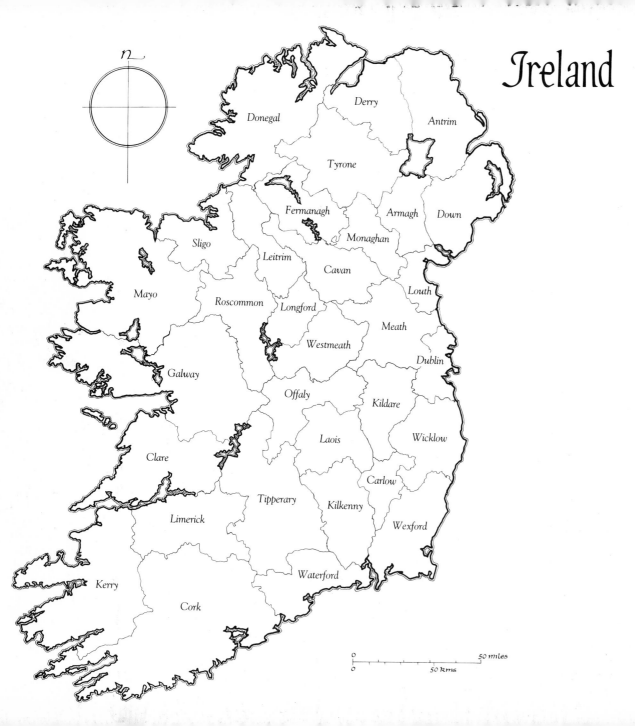

Ireland

N

Donegal

Derry

Antrim

Tyrone

Fermanagh

Armagh

Down

Monaghan

Sligo

Leitrim

Cavan

Louth

Mayo

Roscommon

Longford

Meath

Westmeath

Dublin

Galway

Offaly

Kildare

Laois

Wicklow

Clare

Carlow

Tipperary

Kilkenny

Limerick

Wexford

Kerry

Waterford

Cork

Opposite Near Brandon, Co. Kerry.

0   50 miles

0   50 kms

*P*assage East on the triple estuary of the rivers Barrow, Suir and Nore – not by any means to be confused with Passage West which has become a rather haughty residential suburb of Cork on the estuary of the Lee – is the epitome of the maritime village. All the visual clichés abound – 'narrow winding streets', 'picturesque harbour views', 'bustling quayside'. A ferry plies to the twin villages of Arthurstown and Ballyhack on the Wexford bank. Passage East itself guards the Waterford side – though not with complete success, since we may recall that Richard de Clare ('Strongbow') landed here with a force in 1170, and that Henry II with 4,000 men and 400 ships (can we believe the statistic?) did the same a year later.

South of the village, on a craggy summit, stands Geneva Barracks – all that remains to tell the tale of an idealistic but ill-fated proposal in 1784 to establish a free city which would receive immigrant democrats from Geneva, where the followers of Rousseau and the Enlightenment were feeling the sting of a bourgeois backlash. The idea was that the craftsmen in the group would set up a watchmaking industry in Ireland; fifty houses would be built to accommodate them and eventually, as the city dedicated to the principles of liberty grew, a university would be built to attract scholars and students from all over Europe. It was, unfortunately, an impracticable dream, and it came to nothing in spite of initial optimism in Ireland and Switzerland. The quiet domesticity of the streets of Passage East today contrasts wildly with the grandiose 18th-century plans for boulevards, vistas and collegiate quadrangles.

Many flour-mills were established in the south-east of Ireland during the late 18th and early 19th centuries, often by Quaker families who possessed a genuine desire to improve the quality of life in the district by giving fair employment. Sturdy, unpretentious houses, built for the owner or mill-manager, are still to be seen beside slow-flowing streams, particularly in the counties watered by the tributaries of the rivers Blackwater, Suir, Nore, Barrow and Slaney. Most of the mills have recently fallen into ruin because of the centralization of the grain industry.

Dunmore East is situated five miles south of Passage East, where the Suir estuary opens into the broad ocean. Its harbour has been hugely expanded in recent years to accommodate one of the largest fishing fleets in Western Europe.

Sociologists – if there are any in the neighbourhood – would certainly appreciate the heterogeneous 'mix' in the population: the long-established families, who gain their living from the sea; the professional-class commuters who prefer the life of this kind of community to Waterford's suburbia; and the retired folk, lured back, perhaps, by memories of childhood holidays with bucket and spade in the abundance of sandy coves, cliff-top walks with bouncy spaniels and ozone-sniffing great-aunts, and blackberrying picnics among the salt-bitten hedgerows.

*C*astletownshend typifies for many people the physical manifestations of the Anglo-Irish enclave: the Big House, the neatly organized street, the moored yachts; architecture is provided by the Church of Ireland; and on winter afternoons there is the unmistakably sweet cry of the hounds.

As it happens, there are several Big Houses in this neighbourhood. The grandest is *The Castle*, situated right on the shore of Castle Haven, and home of the Townshend family – George Bernard Shaw married one of them, Charlotte, and called her 'my Irish millionairess'. At the upper end of the village is the four-square Irish-Georgian *Drishane*, the Somerville home. Edith OEnone Somerville was co-author, with her cousin Violet Martin ('Martin Ross'), of several Big House novels, the best of which is *The Real Charlotte* (no intentional aspersions on Mrs Shaw), one of the truly great works of Anglo-Irish prose fiction. Their short stories, running to many series and entitled *Experiences of an Irish R.M.*, were – and still are – exceedingly popular and have never been out of print. Read them, and discover how much more perceptive, sensitive and witty they are than the television series allowed many millions of viewers to take them to be.

In St Barrahane's Church there are monuments to generations of distinguished Somervilles, Townshends, Chavasses and Coghills, as well as fine stained glass, woodwork and embroidery.

West of Skibbereen – if you can tear yourself away from Mrs Salter-Townshend's baronial guest-house in Castletownshend (*left*) – is Ballydehob, the 'Town of Two Mouths', for the River Rathruane divides in two after it foams out from the long stone bridge by which traffic enters the village. The 'new' (19th-century) main street takes you in a gentle curve round the side of a hill: the older street climbs breathlessly to the top and then lets you down rather dangerously onto the Schull road. It is the newer street which gives Ballydehob its eloquence – a rising crescent of small houses and shops with varnished wooden fascias and nameboards supported by wonderfully carved consoles. Here the West Cork tradition of strong exterior colours is never seen to better advantage than on a damp wintry afternoon when the contrast with grey-green nature raises the spirits no end. The pub interiors behind these joyous façades (like that of Nell and Julia Levis, *above*) are similarly warm and welcoming.

$\mathcal{B}$altimore, which gave its name to a city in Maryland, is a fishing and boatbuilding village on the populous coast of West Cork. It is the embarkation point for nearby Sherkin Island and also for the six-mile crossing to Ireland's most southerly territory, Clear Island – or Oileán Cléire as it is still called, for the inhabitants are fastidious Irish-speakers.

Baltimore is full of colour and interest. In the summer, when yachting parties put in for the night – often, no doubt, extending their stay to several days – and other people come to buy new boats or have older ones repaired, a highly cosmopolitan atmosphere prevails. Old salts, jack tars and jolly mariners abound: a convivial scene.

In 1631 Baltimore was raided by pirates from Algiers who killed those inhabitants whom they did not abduct as slaves. The 19th-century poet Thomas Davis wrote stirringly of the event in *The Sack of Baltimore*:

Oh! some must tug the galley's oar, and some must tend the steed –
This boy will bear a Sheik's chibouk, and that a Bey's jereed;
Oh! some are for the arsenals by beauteous Dardanelles,
And some are for the caravan to Mecca's sandy dells . . .

This traditional hearth (*left*), hospitably flanked by its topiary arm-chairs, gives humorous distinction to a West Cork garden. The village of Rosscarbery itself, with its spacious central square enclosed by several gems of 19th-century shopfront design – collectors's pieces, even if some are not in the best repair – is full of interest and charm. It was once a much more important place, through the fame of its 6th-century monastery.

In the 12th-century Rosscarbery was raised to the status of Bishopric. Now, both Church of Ireland and Roman Catholic bishops live elsewhere, for the southern diocese have been rearranged, but vestigial memories of ecclesiastical magnificence linger. The local saint, Fachtna, is honoured by both religions in the dedication of the parish churches.

Courtmacsherry is a quiet village a little further west, on the shores of the bay of the same name. The neighbourhood is rich in interesting historical sites, the most splendid being the Franciscan friary of Timoleague, founded in 1312 by Dónal Mór MacCarthy and greatly added to by Edmond de Courcy (Bishop of Ross) in the early 16th century. There are several MacCarthy castles nearby.

Fionn Tráigh – Anglicized and abbreviated to Ventry – means
Beautiful Strand: but one does not need a knowledge of the Irish
language to appreciate what is obvious to the eye. Ventry village (*above*) is
on the southern side of the incomparable Dingle Peninsula. Dunquin
(*right*) stands at its tip, facing out to the now depopulated Blasket Islands.

Dunquin lies in country rich in myth, folklore and memories of a
turbulent and tragic past; and rich in archaeological and architectural
reminders of that past. The area is still Irish-speaking, and proudly so.
Schoolchildren come from all parts of Ireland to the summer language
schools; older scholars come from all over the world to study the language
– the earliest 'modern' language in Europe into which, for example, the
Aeneid was translated.

During the early years of this century three remarkable books emerged from the Blasket islands – off Slea Head and near Dunquin – to become bestsellers in the bookshops of Manhattan and Mayfair: *An Old Woman Remembers* by Peig Sayers, *The Islandman* by Tomás O'Criomhthain, and *Twenty Years a-Growing* by Muiris O'Suilleabháin – works coaxed out of their authors and translated into English by sympathetic foreign hands.

The playwright John Millington Synge spent some time here:

Bring Kateen-Beug and Maurya Jude
To dance in Beg-Innish,
And when the lads (they're in Dunquin)
Have sold their crabs and fish,
Wave fawny shawls and call them in,
And call the little girls who spin,
And seven weavers from Dunquin,
To dance in Beg-Innish . . .

*I*nch, location for the shooting of the film of Synge's *The Playboy of the Western World*, is one of two great strands at the head of Dingle Bay. It runs for three miles, backed by sandhills, and in the far distance are the ever-changing shapes of the Macgillycuddy Reeks, Ireland's highest mountains.

As everywhere on the Dingle Peninsula, there are numerous ancient sites and curious stone artefacts: a ring-fort at Doonclaur, a tumulus at Knockane, a cross-pillar at Gortacurraun, Ogham stones at Rathduff and Ballinahunt, and a Knights of Kerry castle at Minard.

Annacotty, like many another village in Limerick and surrounding counties, has its annual gymkhana, at which the supremacy of the Horse in Ireland is triumphantly demonstrated. You may be sure that the youngest of this trio (*left*) – in spite of the absence of conventional habiliments – is as much at home in the horse world as the smartly turned-out lady and gentleman in the foreground.

Adare, by the River Maigue (*left*) and scene of a game and country fair (*right*), is known as 'the most beautiful village in Ireland'. It is paradoxically, extremely English-looking: a superb example of the *cottage orné* type of rustic architecture; and this is because an early 19th-century landlord, the third Earl of Dunraven, was inspired by what his relatives were doing for their tenants west of the Cotswolds. Thatched eaves, lattice-work, box hedges, hollyhocks and tea-shoppes abound. Shortly after the foundation of the new Irish state a highly enterprising Local Authority laid out a scheme of new council houses in a sympathetic style. Adare, of course, is much older than all this, as five magnificent buildings testify. The 13th-century Desmond Castle and the 15th-century Franciscan Friary on the banks of the River Maigue are now in ruins – but well-preserved ruins. The 14th-century Augustinian Abbey by the Maigue bridge was restored as a Protestant church and school in 1822, a rather remarkable undertaking in those days; but even more remarkable was the restoration, also inspired by the Dunraven family, of the 13th-century Trinitarian Abbey in the main street as a Roman Catholic parish church. Lastly, Adare Manor, erstwhile home of the Dunravens, is a vast country house in a kind of hybrid Gothic style rarely found in Ireland. It was started in 1822 by the Pain brothers of Cork, and continued by P.C. Hardwick (who provided some handsome buildings for the nearby city of Limerick) and A.W. Pugin. Pugin's interiors are splendidly baronial and draughty.

There really are mines at Silvermines, worked sporadically over the last few hundred years with varying degrees of success dependant upon the introduction of successive new technologies. The village, which could by no stretch of the imagination be classed as 'industrial', is situated where the pastures of Tipperary start rising up to meet the Silvermine Mountains.

The upward curve of the graph of landscape is so gentle you hardly realize you are climbing until you are suddenly walking in bracken and furze, your breath a few yards behind you, while the grey slate roofs start to merge with the greens of field and hedgerow below.

Looking further to the west there is the silver flash of the River Shannon emerging from Lough Derg, the lake mostly hidden by the Ara Mountains, themselves merging into the Aughty Mountains of Co. Clare. The highest point behind you – if you are looking out over Silvermines towards Clare – is Keeper Hill, a great brown hump like a stranded whale. It dominates the county.

Kilaloe is known today chiefly as a haven for boating enthusiasts on the inland waterways – but it is impossible even on the most perfunctory stroll from cabin-cruiser to grocery-store or pub not to be made vividly aware of two thousand years of history. Down in the water meadows, near where the lordly Shannon leaves Lough Derg, are the earthen ramparts of Brian Boru's fort – a site which archaeologists claim had been in existence from Bronze Age times. High above the town was Kincora, Brian's royal palace:

> O where, Kincora, is Brian the Great,
> And where is the beauty that once was thine?

sang the 11th-century poet MacLiag, in nostalgic vein.

The cathedral (seat of the Church of Ireland bishop) is named in honour of St Flannan, and was founded by Dónal Mór O'Brien in the 12th century. Its dark echoing interior, much more spacious than the rather modest exterior would lead one to expect, is full of fascinating pieces of sculpture of many periods, the most marvellous being the richly carved Hiberno-Romanesque doorway, and the oddest the 'Thurgin stone' which has both Ogham and Runic inscriptions. 'St Flannan's Oratory' in the grounds is not in fact an oratory at all, but a small stone-roofed church. St Molua's Oratory – Kilaloe, or 'Cill Molua', takes its name from this saint – beside the Roman Catholic church, was removed from Friary Island in 1929 when the Shannon Hydro Electric Scheme caused the level of the river and lake to rise uncomfortably high. The builders of the Shannon Scheme were also responsible for creating the wide new canal. The 18th-century Grand Canal Company built a quay here too; it is now a quiet backwater used as moorings by the owners of private craft.

Kilkishen is one of a number of very small villages in East Clare which, throughout their entire history, could have been described, rather plaintively, as 'having seen better days'. But better days have come, fairly recently, and as a result of tourism: not mass tourism, but tourism of the kindlier nature which includes Farmhouse Holidays, Archaeological Study Camps and the highly successful 'Rent an Irish Cottage' scheme.

None of this could have happened without Shannon Airport (10 miles away), from which mass tourism of a certain kind may be said to originate; but the authorities have taken extreme care not to destroy the intimacy of the surroundings by encouraging more visitors to places like Kilkishen, Bodyke, Quin, Feakle and Broadford than is patently good for them. Large numbers of visitors can be catered for in the hotels of Limerick, or at the banquet entertainments of Bunratty Castle.

*W*est Clare – with its immense skies and wide horizons – is as different from East Clare as the cities of Belfast and Cork are from one another. Long, low houses manage to sustain the buffeting of the Atlantic winds, from which (it is related) seven dishevelled Spanish Armada ships took refuge at Carrigaholt in 1588. Another ran aground in Doonbeg river, and three more off Quilty (the headland is now known as 'Spanish Point'). A local landlord, Turlough O'Brien, organized his tenants into preventing the sailors from landing – which rather disposes of the theory that the dark-haired people of the western coast are the descendants of shipwrecked Spaniards.

At Mountshannon we are back in East Clare again, leafy and luxuriant, close to the verdant edge of Lough Derg. Visitors are urged to hire a rowing-boat – or, indeed, a motor-boat if time is short, though one should not hurry through this scenic land – to Holy Island, where there is a very well-preserved round tower and the interesting remains of St Caimin's monastery. Whether the passer-by is interested in history and archaeology or not, the setting itself is a delight.

*C*lifden is, historically speaking, an artificial town. It was created by the philanthropic John Darcy in the early 19th century to be a marketing and fishing centre for Iar Connacht, that montainous sea-indented region of hamlets and small scatterings of habitation. Today, no place could seem less artificial: the tall houses in the main street, and the smaller houses of the side streets, are all built in the local stone and dressed in the traditional stucco and brightly coloured paints. There is a weathered feeling, too, as if the buildings had been present for several centuries.

The two churches have only been present for little more than 150 years, but they do not look at all imposed. Their tall spires echo and complement the precipitous heights of the Twelve Bens (sometimes called the Twelve Pins) which form a background of rock and heather, ever-changing in the extraordinary and unique light of this most westerly point of Europe. Only two buildings in the town are out of place – a new and glassy hotel, and a not-so-new motel which strikes a discordant note as you arrive from the Galway road; both emphasize the fact that the principal industry now is tourism – but the other hotels and guest-houses, old and new, manage to blend with the surroundings.

Clifden is famous for the Connemara Pony Show in August – an event visited by enthusiasts who come in every sort of equipage from the ass-and-cart to the Rolls-Royce. An intriguing cross-section of Irish (and international) society may be seen. Porter, whiskey and champagne are shared on the fair green.

There are wonderful small shops selling tweed and handknits, and, strangely enough, the best doughnuts in the world. Margaret Joyce (*left*) runs a drapery business; like many of the other small shops, hers gives character to the street. The Joyces are also famous for their music: as one local man put it, 'The Joyces of Connemara! You'd walk twenty miles up to your waist in snow to hear one of them sing!'

*O*ughterard and Roundstone in Co. Galway are both considered by discriminating visitors (and settlers) to represent the pith or kernel of Western Irishness. Such a view is not shared precisely by the indigenous. Roundstone was created by a Scotsman, one Alexander Nimmo, who was engaged on marine engineering works along the coast in the early 19th century and who in fact was responsible for the settlement of enterprising Scots fishermen. Roundstone therefore became a small English-speaking district in the middle of the Gaeltacht, and indeed the Anglicization of the original place-name, Cloch na Rón, shows the settlers' impatience with the Irish language: although 'cloch' does indeed mean 'stone', 'rón' has nothing to do with 'round', for a rón is a seal; and so this village should have been more correctly designated Seal's Stone.

A different class of settler inhabits Oughterard, an inland village on the road from Galway City to Clifden and Roundstone. He (and she) tend to wear very good Irish tweeds, homeknits and stout leather brogues, but their accents betray an upbringing in Hants or Bucks, or perhaps the Dublin suburb of Killiney, with at least four years at an English public school. These people, seeking simplicity, have brought sophistication – to which the stocks of good wines, patés and Huntley & Palmer biscuits in the local grocery stores testify. Such settlers are, by nature, also good conservationists, and so there has been rather less damage to the local environment in this neighbourhood than in other parts of Ireland.

*L*etterfrack in West Connemara is associated in the Irish mind with a large Reformatory for wayward boys – all too grim a presence in so picturesque a landscape. The Reformatory buildings now, more happily, house an adventurous Craft Centre. The Kylemore State Forest provides a spectacular background. Kylemore Abbey was built by a rich Liverpudlian, Mr Mitchell Henry, as an expensive rural retreat, to a design by J. F. Fuller (who was also the architect of Ashford Castle, Co. Mayo). Far from creating an inappropriate eyesore, the Victorian Gothic 'abbey' gives point to the grandeur of the scene.

The wonderfully secluded harbour of Cleggan nearby is the place from which you take the motorboat – or hooker, if you are lucky, and romantically disposed – to Inishbofin (Inis Bó Finne: the Island of the Beautiful Cow). The poet Richard Murphy lives at Cleggan; several of his major works, such as *The Last Galway Hooker, Sailing to an Island* and *The Cleggan Disaster*, are inspired by incidents and traditions of this neighbourhood. Inishbofin was 'discovered' by tourists in the 1960s, but their numbers are not all that great and the island is still a perfect retreat for an utterly peaceful holiday. Colman, Bishop of Lindisfarne, established a monastery here in order to get away from it all, following the Synod of Whitby in 663. Cromwell had a different attitude to isolation: he used the island as a concentration camp – but no pernicious atmosphere remains. In summer, there is a Mediterranean quality in the brilliant light and the vivid blue of the sea.

Killary Harbour is eight miles long and only a hundred yards wide in some places. It is said by some geographers to be the only true fjord in Ireland: others declare it to be a drowned valley. During the 1914-1918 war it was proposed that the entire British navy could take refuge there, if required – the occasion did not arise for so vast an undertaking, though some ships did put in.

Leenane sits on the southern shore of the harbour, where roads to Westport, Clifden and Maam meet. There is an attractive, old-established hotel – the only building of note. A couple of miles away, at the head of the fjord, the Eriff River splashes into the sea under an old stone bridge. Mweelrea Mountain dominates the surrounding scenery, which is spectacular, whichever road you choose.

Achill is the largest of Ireland's offshore islands. It is reached by a bridge at Achill Sound, so you are hardly aware that you are on an island at all. Within its 50-mile perimeter it contains some of the most magnificent cliffs in Ireland (Meenaun), superb beaches (Keel, Dooagh, Keem and Dugort), a mountain (Slievemore) from which literally breathtaking views of the Mayo coast from Blacksod Bay to Clew Bay may be seen, a corry or glacial lake (Acorrymore), a deserted 'famine' village and several prehistoric graves and standing stones.

During the 1830s a clergyman, the Rev E. Nangle, established a mission in order to convert the starving Roman Catholic islanders; his efforts were largely in vain, and Protestantism has sustained a rather poor press locally ever since. A tyrant of a secular kind, Captain Boycott, lived for a time at Corrymore House, run a century later as a guesthouse by the totally untyrannical yet eccentric Major Dermot Freyer, a journalist and short-story writer who charged nothing to guests who interested him, but quite a lot to those whom he found boring. The painter Paul Henry lived in Achill during one of his most productive periods in the 1910s and 20s.

Many of the mid-20th century dwellings on the island are built of concrete, with flat roofs reminiscent of north Africa as depicted in Cubist art. Crenellations in concrete blocks are a feature. The cottage at Drummin (*right*) is older and, one would think, cosier in the north Atlantic climate.

Mrs Alice Kerrigan (*left*) keeps a traditional drapery store in Louisburgh, Co. Mayo (would that all the shops in Irish villages retained such an air of friendliness and intimacy!). Louisburgh is called after Louise Browne, a beautiful 18th-century member of a family which is still important in the neighbourhood. Croagh Patrick, Ireland's holy mountain, dominates this countryside.

Killala is famous for the landing of the French force in 1798 – the most substantial manifestation of Napoleon's interest in the United Irish insurrection. As a result of the filming of a television serial based on Thomas Flanagan's novel *The Year of the French*, all 20th-century street furniture, such as telegraph poles and electricity standards, was removed from the streets, improving the townscape immeasurably.

Fermanagh is known as 'Ulster's lakeland' – about a quarter of the surface of the county is water. The River Erne, with its two great lakes and countless tributaries, is the reigning genius of the place.

Kesh is at the centre of one of the most interesting areas of Fermanagh. Famous for fishing and boating, it is also a convenient point from which to explore the Castle Archdale forest park and Crevenish, a 'planter' castle erected by Sir Thomas Blennerhassett of Norfolk in the early 17th century; but by far the most extraordinary sights are to be seen on the Boa and White islands. On the former there are two grotesque stone figures, undoubtedly pre-Christian; on the latter, eight stone figures, now reassembled and mounted in the wall of an early Christian church.

Derrylin is a pleasant village close to Upper Lough Erne. This neighbourhood, a maze of rivers and small lakes, has many old graveyards where a macabre design of stone sculpture may be seen, incorporating skull, crossbones and hourglass. The most important is at Galloon Island near the confluence of the Erne and Finn rivers, about six miles from Derrylin. In the village are two stone heads, probably of much later date, painted in bright colours – no doubt in order to amuse.

Killybegs (*right*) is noted for its fishing fleet and its carpet making: industries based on the natural resources of ocean and moorland. It is a village full of enterprise and bustle – none of the jaded introspection which is to be found further south. Things get done in Killybegs, yet there is always time for 'a bit of crack' – a word which suggests a sharpness of mind and tongue. Mountcharles (*left*) has a different character: a small and rather rundown village on the road from Donegal town, ancestral home of the Conyngham family.

Teelin and Malinbeg are as remote as you could wish, situated east and west, respectively, of the immense Slieve League cliffs, and looking across 15 miles of ocean to Ben Bulben, Sligo's mythic mountain.

The Co. Donegal poet William Allingham (1824-89) captured some of the magic of the place in a poem called *The Fairies*, still learned by every Irish schoolchild:

High on the hilltop
The old king sits;
He is now so old and grey
He has nigh lost his wits.
With a bridge of white mist
Columbkille he crosses,
On his stately journeys
From Slieveleague to Rosses;
Or going up with music
On cold starry nights,
To sup with the queen
Of the gay northern lights . . .

*C*olm Chille – 'the Dove of the Church', otherwise known as St Columba – was born in Co. Donegal, the son of a princely house. The glen which bears his name faces west into the Atlantic, and is very much a community on its own, cut off from the rest of the county by a semi-circle of mountains.

The now almost legendary Fr James McDyer started a co-operative scheme here in the 1950s and 60s in an effort to stem the flow of emigration and to give the parish the kind of pride which can only proceed from self-help. One of the most successful projects was the building of holiday cottages in traditional style. Visitors to these cottages are encouraged to take part in the day-to-day activities of village life. There is also a hotel, some pubs, and plenty of spectacular walks and fine strands. There are also several ring-forts, incised pillar-stones, a cairn, and a prehistoric chamber-tomb: but the lasting impression is one of a dauntless and friendly people.

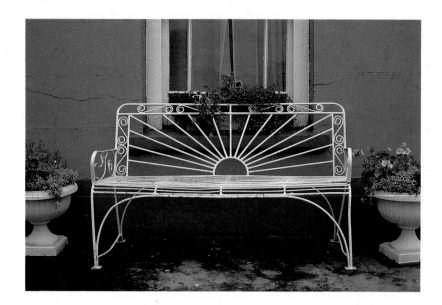

The road from Glencolumbkille ascends steeply through Glengesh Pass and descends again to Ardara at the mouth of the Owentocker river. Like most of the villages in this part of Donegal, Ardara exports tweed and handknits to the boutiques of the fashionable world.

Glenties, five miles to the north, is a neat village which has often won the Irish Tourist Board's coveted Tidy Towns award. There is a very fine Roman Catholic church designed by Liam McCormick of Derry, consecrated in 1976 – one of a number by the same architect in this diocese.

The Gaeltacht, or Irish-speaking, district of Donegal is surprisingly densely populated, the houses seeming to grow out of the land like the hummocks and boulders. The farms in Rosbeg are brightly painted, with trim gardens displaying a greater pride in place (and of persons) than is always the case in similar areas elsewhere. The Ulster countryfolk – for Donegal is part of the old province, even though politically situated in the Republic – always show great interest in affairs outside their own locality, and are exceedingly hospitable to the casual visitor, while never losing any of their own natural dignity.

*N*orth Donegal's coastline is made up of a bewildering array of high headlands, vast sweeping strands, deep indentations peppered with islets, and sunken valleys resembling fjords – Lough Swilly is two-dozen miles long from its Atlantic mouth to the quay of Letterkenny. Dunfanaghy looks across its strand on an inlet of Sheephaven at Horn Head, where there is a switchback road, quite terrifying to the unwary motorist.

*C*arrowkeel (or Kerrykeel) is a village on the edge of one of these inlets – the magnificent Mulroy Bay, which snakes its way south from the sea at Melmore Head and Ballyhooriskey Point to the well-set-up town of Milford. Knockalla Hill, behind the village, is celebrated in the world of motor sport for the arduous and eccentric 'Knockalla Hill Climb'. At less noisy moments the panorama of North Donegal may be sublimely assimilated.

Rathmullen is rather smart: this is not the Donegal of crags and cottages, of cliffs and kittiwakes and crochet made by crooked fingers by lamplight. If the busy people of Glenties take pleasure in making carpets, the people of Rathmullen (and Ramelton, too, no doubt – see p. 68) probably take pleasure in buying them.

It was from Rathmullen in 1607 that the Earls of Tyrone and Tirconnell sailed for Europe, signifying the end of the old Gaelic order. The incident has become known as the 'Flight of the Earls', and much sad poetry has been written about it and about the subsequent decline of Gaelic Ireland. Curiously enough, Ulster had remained the last bastion of this culture – but the systematic settlement of Scots and English throughout the 17th century ensured that Gaelic Ireland would never again predominate.

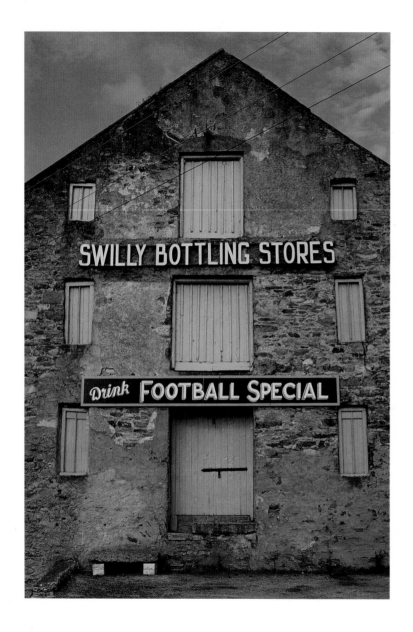

Ramelton, six miles south of Rathmullen, also brings those who enjoy an attractive streetscape; there is none of the almost inevitable sense of decay associated with so many of Ireland's older towns and villages. Retired people often settle here.

The warehouses are splendid – few of them used for their original industrial purposes (brewing, linen manufacture, flour milling), yet many successfully adapted to other uses, and some very sympathetically restored. The quayside, with its sturdy mercantile buildings, and bold use of colour, is particularly arresting.

Though there are scatterings and clusters of houses north of Malin, this village can probably claim to be the most northerly one of any significant size in Ireland. Malin Head is Ireland's most northerly point.

The village has a prosperous air. From it, short excursions can be made to various vantage-points on the Head, from which only half-a-century ago a popular pastime was the identification of the great liners which passed to and fro, on the route from Liverpool and Glasgow to Quebec, Halifax, Boston and New York.

Nearer to home and a few miles inland, at Carndonagh, is the splendid incised cross of St Patrick, as well as two incised flanking stones, and a superby carved pillar-stone.

*C*uldaff, Moville and Greencastle (p. 74) are all villages on the eastern side of Inishowen – that great peninsula which has Malin Head at its tip. Inishowen is almost a county in itself. The name suggests that it is an island ('inish') and early seafarers, anxiously sounding the intricacies of Loughs Swilly and Foyle to west and east, may well have believed that this was so. Yet Inishowen is an island in another sense, for its people consider themselves as being somewhat apart from the rest of Donegal. Culdaff has a pleasant beach. There is a rock in the Culdaff River known as 'St Bodan's Boat' in which that saint was miraculously conveyed to Scotland – and, presumably, back again.

*M*oville was a calling-point for ships on the North Atlantic route. Many local songs and poems tell of departures: their theme is that of the emigrant's farewell to his native land. Moville is less than 20 miles from Derry City – in Northern Ireland, but still regarded as the capital of the region, whichever side of the political border you happen to come from.

Greencastle looks across the mouth of Lough Foyle at Magilligan Point and the magnificent five-mile strand beyond. The castle which dominates the village is of Anglo-Norman origin, with many later additions including a 19th-century artillery fort which is now part of a hotel. The castle changed hands and allegiances many times, reflecting the vagaries of Irish history. The Norman De Burgos lost it to Edward Bruce (Robert's brother) and his Irish allies, regained it, and lost it again. It was occupied by the O'Dohertys in Elizabethan times, but was captured by the English after the Flight of the Earls (see p. 66), and remained a bastion of the Ulster Plantation until a more recent political change placed it in the sympathetic care of the National Monuments division of the Irish Office of Public Works.

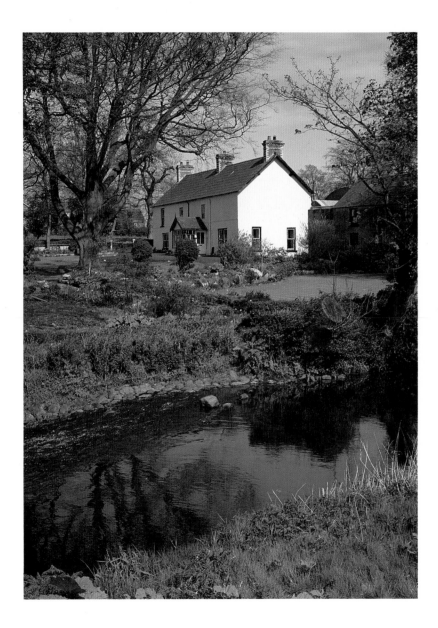

Whiskey connoisseurs require no introduction to Bushmills, for whiskey has been distilled here under licence since 1608. The fine 'Old Bushmills' distillery, with its Pot Still bar, may be visited at advertised times – the oldest whiskey distillery in the British Isles, and therefore in the world!

The Bush River has been the local source of energy for centuries. A remarkable example was the harnessing of its power in 1883 to provide electricity for the electric tramway which transported sightseers from Portrush to the Giant's Causeway. The tramway survived until 1950, when the company was forced to close because impatient tourists preferred their own cars.

There are a number of interesting architectural features in and around the village – Billy Church, the Georgian Dundarave House, water-mills, old stone bridges, and a 19th-century clock tower which resembles an old Irish round tower.

Ballynure, near the town of Ballyclare, is pleasantly placed on the Ballynure Water. There is a forge nearby, where the blacksmith still shoes the horses of the local yeomanry, gentry and aristocracy.

The bracken up the braeside has rusted in the air,
The birch trees lean together, so silver-tongued and fair . . .

So runs the *Song of Glendun*, by the local poet Moira O'Neill, who died in 1956. Cushendun village lies at the foot of Glendun where the brown Glendun river meets the aquamarine of the Moyle, that white-flecked sea which divides Antrim from Kintyre and which is described all too prosaically on the map as the North Channel. Scotland is only 17 miles away, and there is hardly a day in the year when you cannot see some hill of Galloway or Arran from Cushendun Bay. It is no wonder that the earliest exchanges between Britain and Ireland took place across this neck of sea, or that words usually assumed to be Scots – such as 'brae' quoted in the song – are also claimed for this part of Ireland. The houses of Cushendun are neat and high-gabled, topped by watery grey slates: the National Trust now has proprietary rights to the village and its pine-fringed strand – as well it might.

The windswept verge of the North Antrim plateau, with its high skies and clear light, ends – harmlessly enough, one would think – in broad fields of wheat and turnips. Move closer, and you are suddenly on the edge of sheer cliffs of volcanic rock, with sharp spikes of stone jutting up from the swirling waters below. Beside Ballintoy Church a half-hidden corkscrew road takes you down to Ballintoy Harbour, a rock-enclosed pool strangely calm in the noise of the surf outside the reef. Near here one of the ships of the Spanish Armada was pounded against the rocks; its treasures, recently recovered from the sea-bed, are now in the Ulster Museum. Centuries of immersion have not reduced their glitter. During the rebellion of 1641 Protestants hid in the tower of the church (*right*), fed, it is related, by the local Roman Catholic priest.

Visitors are generally advised to make Cushendall their centre for exploring the Glens of Antrim – but in fact you can start anywhere you please on the Antrim Coast Road and turn inland into whichever glen first takes your fancy. The Coast Road was built in the early 19th century in order to connect the glens (and their people) with the outside world, and also to give some much-needed temporary employment.

The village of Cushendall is very much the work of an 'improving landlord', Francis Turnly, who flourished at the same time as the Coast Road was laid out. His Curfew Tower, designed as a sort of local jail, is the chief building of interest. Just outside the village is Layde Church, which has a 15th-century vaulted tower and contains in its graveyard memorials to the once-powerful MacDonnell family.

You can ascend Glenballyeamon, Glencorp or Glenaan conveniently from the village, preferably on foot if you have time to spare; or, a little further south, Glenariff, which rises up from Red Bay.

lenarm is the seat of the Earls of Antrim. The village, like most of those at the foot of the glens, is the meeting-point of glen and coast roads. Glenarm was founded in the reign of King John. The most celebrated of the present Earl's ancestors was Sorley Buidhe MacDonnell, one of Queen Elizabeth's bitterest and most remorseless enemies; he is sometimes referred to in modern history books as Sorley *Boy* – but the Irish word *buidhe* means flaxen or yellow-haired.

Glenarm Castle is approached from Castle Street over a two-arched bridge and through a menacing Gothic arch with what looks like a portcullis but which on closer inspection reveals itself as a fanciful 19th-century forgery. The castle itself dates from Jacobean times, but has been rebuilt, re-modelled and restored in successive periods. It is, none the less, an imposing and picturesque building, and its situation against wooded slopes is delightful.

Shane the Proud O'Neill (murdered 1636) is buried in the local churchyard. An unusual number of men of idealistic Nationalist outlook have Glenarm associations, including Eoin McNeill, co-founder of the Gaelic League; James McNeill, the first Irish High Commissioner in London; and Roger Casement, the patriot who was executed for his part in the events of 1916. It should be remembered, though, that Ulster remained the most obdurately Gaelic (and Irish-speaking) province until well into the 17th century, and vestiges of this tradition remain.

Jonesborough in South Armagh is only about a mile from the border with the Republic. It is situated in a hummocky region where the land starts to rise to Slieve Gullion, a mountain associated with many mythological tales. A large open-air market (*left*) is held in Jonesborough on Sundays.

There is a lushness about Richhill and its neighbourhood which gives point and meaning to the name. This northern part of Co. Armagh has long been known as 'the orchard of Ireland': to see it during apple-blossom time is a quick way to enchantment. Other fruits are grown, of course; and jams, jellies and preserves are produced commercially and – more deliciously – in the home. The village grew up round the estate of the Richardson family. Edward Richardson MP built the mansion between 1655 and 1696 in the Dutch style which became quite common in Ireland, but of which very few examples now remain.

'Tyrone among the bushes' is one of the least-known counties of Ireland as far as the visitor is concerned – and undeservedly so. The sheer variety of the landscape, from the Sperrin Mountains to the Clogher Valley, from the flat land bordering Lough Neagh (largest lake in the British Isles) to the slow-flowing Mourne, Strule and Foyle (one river: three names), is remarkable.

Gortin and Donaghmore, likewise, are villages so different in character that they might be at opposite ends of the country. Gortin, with its famous glen, lies on the edge of the Sperrins – a wide-streeted village in romantic scenery. The forest park, south of the village, is a wildlife reserve. Beside it is the stretch of road known locally as 'the magnetic mile': a curious optical effect creates the illusion that the road runs uphill – but it is possible to freewheel down it!

Donaghmore, near the large town of Dungannon, is more gentrified – but none the worse for that. There are some neat early- and mid-19th century houses and the remains of a fine 18th-century brewery. A 9th- or 10th-century figured High Cross is preserved in the main street, where the fragments were re-erected from the site of an earlier monastery in 1776. It is adorned with carvings representing scenes from the Old and New Testaments, in two distinct styles, which suggests that the pieces may originally have belonged not to one cross, but two.

Circular groups of trees, like this one near Donaghmore, are to be seen on hilltops all over Ireland. They are usually the sites of 'raths', or ring-forts – in some parts of Ulster they are known as 'forths' – or, less romantically, ancient enclosures for cattle.

Their sylvan appearance today is largely due to the fact that such earthen circles were later thought to have supernatural origins, and that to cultivate – let alone demolish – the banks would disturb the spirits of the erstwhile dwellers; so trees grew up, crowning the hilltops.

One often hears these places described locally as 'fairy forts' – the Irish fairy having the nature of a shade or ghost: nothing at all like the prettier fairies of English storybooks. Aristocratic landowners of the last two centuries sometimes planted ornamental trees round these ring-forts, to beautify the landscape.

*C*aledon is a village in the Armagh countryside, not far from the cathedral city of the same name. Some of its small terraces charmingly echo the grander ones laid out in the city in the early 19th century. The Earls of Caledon were responsible for the creation of the village, and it is superbly maintained.

Caledon House was designed by Thomas Cooley around 1779; the colonnade and domed pavilions were added by John Nash in 1812. There is a Doric column (1840) surmounted by a statue of the second Earl by the Ulster sculptor Thomas Kirk; the column was designed by William Murray, who, like Cooley, is represented in the City of Armagh, where Church of Ireland Primates provided immense patronage for architects at this period.

Field-Marshall Viscount Alexander of Tunis was born in Caledon House.

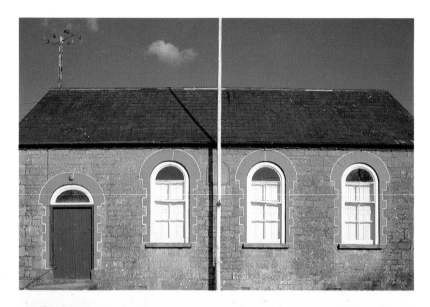

yan is a hamlet in the valley of the Ulster Blackwater between Caledon and Benburb.

This district was an O'Neill stronghold. Sean the Proud O'Neill's castle was burned to the ground in 1566 and the stones are said to have been used by the English to build their fort at Blackwatertown. The English planter, Sir Richard Wingfield, established a new Benburb Castle in the early 16th century, high above the river; it, in turn, was razed by the Irish during the rebellion of 1641. The present Benburb House has become a Priory of the Servites, an order dedicated to serving the community, in this case appropriately in the specific task of reconciliation. The charmingly cultivated estate provides an atmosphere of pastoral peace. It stretches from the river and mill-race to the walls of Kilfeacle Church – the parish is still known by its early Irish name of Kilfeacle, 'fiachail' meaning a tooth. St Patrick is said to have lost a tooth here, and it was preserved as a sacred relic for many years. The village street of Benburb, with its rows of estate cottages, thus runs alongside the gardens and stable yard of what in turn has been known as Castle, House, and Priory.

All roads to Plumbridge pass through valleys of the Sperrins – Butterlope Gap and Barnes Gap are the most spectacular. The Glenelly river (*right*), a tributary of the Foyle, is famous for its trout.

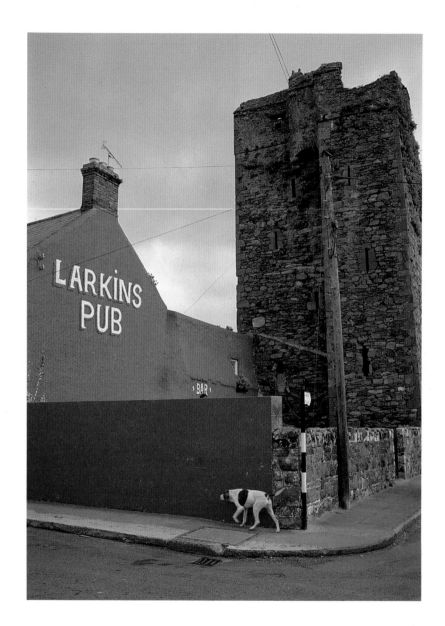

*C*ooley is sometimes described as the 'oldest' part of Ireland. This is because much of Celtic mythology – and especially the Ulster cycle of sagas – originated in this small triangular piece of land betwen two seas. Although the earliest known copy of the most famous story, the Táin Bó Cuailinge ('Cattle Raid of Cooley'), was inscribed in the 7th century, the events chronicled in it had descended in the oral tradition from at least the 1st. The places mentioned are still identified in the names of towns, mountains and rivers. The Táin has been translated by a number of modern poets – that of Thomas Kinsella most effectively distils its magic, its humour and its immediacy.

Carlingford, on Cooley's northern shore, is, of course, a much younger place, as its Viking name suggests. Its street-pattern is a medieval legacy; there are a number of medieval buildings, including a castle named after King John, a tower known as 'the Mint', and another tower which was the residence of the Taafe family.

Gyles' Quay on the lower side of the Cooley peninsula is a minuscule seaside resort, which looks out towards Baile's Strand where Cúchulain, the great Ulster hero of the sagas, fought the waves of the sea and was consumed by them. The Seananda Ballroom is no doubt the scene for another type of romance.

Termonfeckin is celebrated throughout Ireland as the headquarters of the Irish Countrywomen's Association. Newtown House, once the home of the McClintock family, was presented to the I.C.A. by the Kellogg Foundation of the United States, and has been considerably enlarged as a conference centre. Amusing allusions are made by comedians about the nature of the work at Termonfeckin – courses on the manufacture of tea-cosies and seminars on the best ways to cook suet pudding – but this is far from the reality, for the I.C.A. has achieved more than any other organization in improving the quality of rural life.

The village is well kept, and surrounded by fine woods. Its patron is St Fechin, who founded a monastery in the 6th century, of which only a few carved stones remain. Termonfeckin is, surprisingly, situated in the Archbishopric of Armagh, but at its most southerly point, which is probably one of the reasons why the Primates lived here from medieval times until the early 17th century, Armagh being rather remote.

Dunboyne and Duleek are villages in the southern portion of Meath – a rich pastoral county containing the most extraordinary array of architectural masterpieces from 2,500 BC to the last century. The Hill of Tara, seat of the High Kings of Ireland, is situated at its centre. The county is known as 'Royal Meath'.

Dunboyne has suffered somewhat from Dublin's commuter spread, but the centre of the village is virtually unspoiled. There are a number of important stud-farms in the neighbourhood, and Fairyhouse Racecourse is just up the road.

Duleek, a peaceful village further from Dublin, is said to have been founded by St Cianán, who received his bishopric from St Patrick. There are many interesting archaeological remains, including two splendid 10th-century high crosses. Renaissance wayside crosses commemorating the Dowdall family are to be seen in the village and nearby at Athcarne.

irginia in Co. Cavan is the most southerly of the Ulster plantation villages, and is named, appropriately, after the Virgin Queen. The Protestant population has dwindled somewhat since Elizabethan times, but the centrepiece of the village is still the Protestant church, approached by a straight avenue of beautifully clipped yews. An early 19th-century Market House, and some amusingly rusticated cottages, are a feature of the main street.

Duffy (*above right*), or Duff, is a common name in these parts. The neighbouring village of Ballyjamesduff is famous in Irish emigrant communities all over the world for the humorously nostalgic song written by William Percy French, who was, for a time, Inspector of Drains with the Cavan County Council:

There are tones that are tender, and tones that are gruff,
Are whispering over the sea –
Come back, Paddy Reilly, to Ballyjamesduff,
Come home, Paddy Reilly to me . . .

Another common surname is Sheridan (O Sireadáin). General Philip Henry Sheridan, of American Civil War fame, was born near here in 1831. Earlier, the family of Dr Thomas Sheridan lived at Quilca House – a few miles from Virginia – and it was when staying with his friend here that Jonathan Swift started writing *Gulliver's Travels*. Thomas' son, another Thomas, became a well-known actor-manager; and his grandson was Richard Brinsley Sheridan, the playwright.

Granard is dominated by the mote of Hugh de Lacy's castle, and also by the sumptuous Gothic Roman Catholic church designed by John Burke in 1861 which shares the same hilltop. The curving main street leads the eye directly to these monuments. The church, in particular, seems far too grandiose for such a place; but its presence provides a sense of architectural excitement absent in many much larger towns.

Ballyconnell is close to the border with Northern Ireland. It is a busy village with some thriving industries, and an increasingly important role in tourism, for Co. Cavan now attracts large numbers of lake anglers from abroad. In the grounds of the 17th-century Protestant church (*right*) are the outlines of two diamond-shaped fortifications dating from the Williamite wars.

Presbyterian plainness, and plain dealing, in the rural community, reaches as far south as Shercock in Co. Cavan. The roadside 'meeting-houses', plentiful in Armagh and Monaghan, peter out the nearer you get to ultramontane Co. Meath. Although Shercock is dominated by the Church of Ireland tower, and though the majority of the inhabitants favour attendance at the dull Roman Catholic chapel, the Presbyterian church in its lakeside setting is the salient feature seen from all approach roads.

Shercock, in fiction, was the scene of the 'eating house' in Patrick Kavanagh's novel *Tarry Flynn* (1948), where Mrs Flynn unsuccessfully tried to set up her unmarriageable daughters in the hope that they might entice strong farmers on fair days by the lure of their home cooking; alas, their corned beef, spuds and boiled cabbage drew no takers (in any sense), and their catering business was a failure from the start.

Roundwood is said to be the highest village in Ireland; no other village in the much more mountainous regions of Kerry or Donegal seems to have put forward a rival claim. It is situated on the road from Dublin to Glendalough, and for two centuries has been a favourite stopping-point for trippers on their way to see the magical lakes and ruins. (Prior to this, trippers would have been described as 'wayfarers'.)

Avoca, further south, is an extremely picturesque village celebrated by Tom Moore in his poem 'The Meeting of the Waters':

There is not in this wide world a valley so sweet
As the vale in whose bosom the bright waters meet . . .

There is a flourishing handknit and weaving industry; and there has been, from time to time, a great deal of mining in the neighbourhood, the scars of which are not easily obliterated.

*I*t would not have been unusual to find a 'Coach Factory' in a village the size of Dunlavin (*right*) as late as the Second World War, as indeed in any rural community so well supplied with big estates – the highly social landed gentry constantly visiting one another in carriages, phaetons, landaus, broughams, victorias, governess-carts, traps and sidecars: only the last named peculiar to Ireland. The Worth-Tynte family lived hereabouts, and in 1743 Sir Jones Worth-Tynte commissioned the erection of the Dunlavin Court and Market House, possibly from the architect Richard Castle. This building, only extraordinary because of its grandeur in so bucolic a setting, has a masonry dome and Doric columns.

It would be unfair to Rathvilly (*above*) to compare it in architectural splendours with Dunlavin, for Dunlavin is extraordinary; but Rathvilly has a fine church, the tower of which echoes that of Cobden's Carlow Cathedral a few miles away; and the Disraeli School, designed by Welland in 1826, is very charming.

Wayside shrines in Ireland are not as common as they used to be – if we except the large and hideous Marian Year shrines which were built with the pennies of the poor on approach roads to towns in 1954, and in which outsize holy statues stand uncomfortably in a wilderness of dwarf palms, plaster urns and wrought iron. Here in Hacketstown, by contrast, these small domestic shrines are lovingly tended, surrounded by hardy annuals grown from seed-packets. Hacketstown witnessed two battles during the Rising of 1798. Much of the local folklore, here and in the neighbouring county of Wexford, relates to the bravery of the insurgents of that time.

*T*oo many motorists rush through Cullahill in their eagerness to get from Dublin to Cork – the temptation for speeding is great because the road is very good and the village street is wide. If you pause, there are pleasant cottage gardens, and views of farmyards with the wide fields of Laois beyond. There are pubs, and an excellent restaurant. The 15th-century castle of the MacGiolla Phádraig family is really a tower house – most Irish 'castles' are tower houses, a form of fortified dwelling popular in towns as well as in very remote places. There are two other tower houses near Cullahill, at Kilbreedy and Gortnaclea, and it is worth counting the farms in this area where the buildings are clearly centred on the remains of a tower house.

*A*chaidh Ur really means 'Fresh Field', and Freshford is one of many examples of how names of villages and townlands have been changed due to faulty Anglicization. The confusion here is between the words Achaidh (a field) and Ath (a ford). There is no ford in Freshford, but the fields, and the village itself, are as fresh as anything you can imagine. St Lachtain, who died in 622, was Bishop here, and the present church stands on the site of a smaller one which he built. Its Hiberno-Romanesque porch (c. 1100) is very fine. There is an inscribed prayer for the two donors, and also for the sculptor, Gilla Mo-Cholmoc O Cenncucain, one of the very few early artists who has not remained anonymous. The intricately worked silver Shrine of St Lachtain's Arm is now preserved in the Royal Irish Academy. The arm, however, is no longer in it – but if it ever was, it seems that St Lachtain must have been a very small man indeed.

*B*lackwater stands midway between Kilmuckridge and Curracloe – if that makes you any the wiser. All three are villages on the east coast of Wexford; this county has a south coast as well, for at Carnsore you turn the corner which is the south-east point of Ireland. All three villages have magnificent beaches – but it is hard to see where one ends and the next begins, so you can safely say that between them they share over a dozen miles of strand.

'B un Clóidighe' signifies the foot of the Clody River, where the smaller stream joins the wide and salmon-replete Slaney: 'By the streams of Bunclody, where all pleasures do meet . . .', runs an old song.

It is a well-watered land, a land of fine fields and rich foliage. The village, with its gently rising tree-lined street, is notable for its cobblestoned conduits on either side to take the surface water – these, too, may be referred to fancifully in bad weather as the 'streams of Bunclody'.

For four centuries the village was known as Newtownbarry, after the powerful Barry family. It was the 16th-century James Barry who laid out the street on the edge of his estate. A mile or so downstream in the graveyard of Kilmyshall is the tomb of Eileen Booth, who was the original 'Eileen Aroon' of the 17th-century poet and harper Cearbhall O Dálaigh. When Handel was in Dublin for the first performance of *The Messiah* he declared that he would rather have composed the O Dálaigh tune than anything in his oratorio.

The majority of the houses in Kilmore Quay are thatched. Corrugated iron, a fashionable material in rural Ireland in the period between the wars, and one which was decried by conservationists and nature lovers, is now very rare, and has achieved a curiosity value which almost merits its own preservation orders. The Quay is an important deep-sea fishing centre and one can also take a boat out to the Saltee Islands, a noted bird sanctuary.

You might be excused for supposing that Fethard-on-Sea has nothing to do with the sea at all, for the little creek – which, anyway, is dry at low tide – gives no intimation of the great leagues of strand hidden from the village by ferny hummocks, nor of the pink sandstone cliffs a few hundred yards to the south. The scallop shells with which Mr Jimmy O'Leary (*right*) has artfully decorated his Garage and Filling Station must, however, suggest that the seaside cannot be too far away.

Drive on towards Baginbun Head and, suddenly, the whole seascape opens up before you. It was across this sea that the shiftless Normans came in 1170 from Wales, on the invitation of Diarmuid, King of Leinster, who hoped they would help him to settle a local war: but they quite simply settled. They imposed their laws and customs on the wayward Gaelic people, building castles, founding cities, encouraging commerce:

At the creek of Baginbun
Ireland was lost and won . . .

*S*altmills – there used to be a flourishing export in salt – is a small village near Fethard-on-Sea, situated on the lagoon-like Bannow Bay. Behind the village is Tintern Abbey, founded by William the Marshal, Earl of Pembroke, who made a vow during a stormy sea-crossing that, if spared, he would establish a monastery as an offshoot of Tintern in Monmouthshire. Only romantic vestiges of the Abbey remain, attached to a 19th-century mansion.

*S*lade is on the other side of Fethard-on-Sea, almost at the end of the Hook Head. The castle (*right*) is delightfully placed on the water's brink: however, matters far removed from the charm of the scene were in the minds of the Laffan family who built it as a fortification against maritime marauders in the 15th century. The castle was cruelly wrested from the Laffans at the time of the Cromwellian land confiscation. Slade pier, under the castle walls, is much frequented by boating and fishing enthusiasts.

At Ballyhack on the Wexford bank of the triple estuary of the Barrow, Suir and Nore, we face the village of Passage East – where our journey began (see p. 12) – on the Waterford bank. The castle was a preceptory of the Knights Templar: so much in this region reminds us of the Normans. Three miles to the north are the substantial ruins of Dunbrody Abbey, founded by Cistercians only about a dozen years after the Norman invasion. Further on, at Kilmokea, earthworks may be seen – all that remains of an Anglo-Norman village built a hundred or so years later.

Our tailpiece picture (*turn to p. 128*) is a surprise, for it is most unusual to see a Post Office sign in the English language only: they are normally in English and Irish, though sometimes the English version is omitted. It would be pointless to try and discover the reason for this eccentricity. Subtle answers, such as the suggestion that Rush is a Norse foundation and therefore several centuries removed from the Gaelic nation, are inclined to lead nowhere.

Overleaf Pubs traditional and not-so-traditional in (*top, left to right*) Ballyraggett, Co. Kilkenny (Carney House and Barney's); Ramelton, Co. Donegal; Gortin, Co. Tyrone; and (*bottom, left to right*) Virginia, Co. Cavan; Clifden, Co. Galway; Castleconnell, Co. Limerick; Kilmore Quay, Co. Wexford.

LOUNGE CARNEY HOUSE BAR

BARNEY'S
GUINNESS No beer comes near.

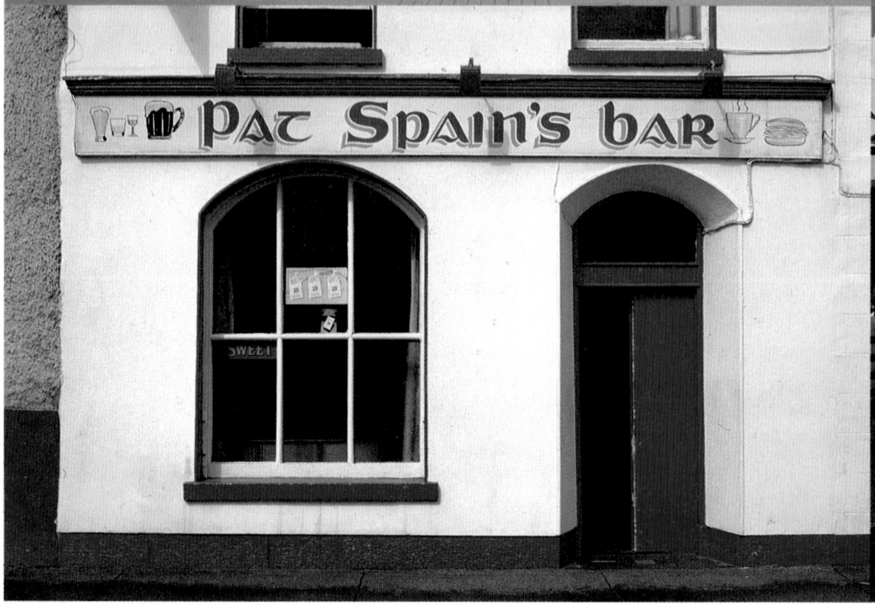
Pat Spain's bar

King's Bar
TOM KING SELECT BAR
MUSIC NIGHT
GUINNESS

Rush, Co. Dublin